Bunk Beds and Apple Boxes

Early Number Sense

Catherine Twomey Fosnot

*first*hand
An imprint of Heinemann
A division of Reed Elsevier, Inc.
361 Hanover Street
Portsmouth, NH 03801–3912
firsthand.heinemann.com

Harcourt School Publishers
6277 Sea Harbor Drive
Orlando, FL 32887–6777
www.harcourtschool.com

Offices and agents throughout the world

ISBN 13: 978-0-325-01006-9
ISBN 10: 0-325-01006-4

ISBN 13: 978-0-15-360558-1
ISBN 10: 0-15-360558-8

© 2007 Catherine Twomey Fosnot

The development of a portion of the material described within was supported in part by the National Science Foundation under Grant No. 9911841. Any opinions, findings, and conclusions or recommendations expressed in these materials are those of the authors and do not necessarily reflect the views of the National Science Foundation.

Library of Congress Cataloging-in-Publication Data
CIP data is on file with the Library of Congress

Printed in the United States of America on acid-free paper

11 10 09 08 07   ML   1 2 3 4 5 6

Acknowledgements

Literacy Consultant

Nadjwa E.L. Norton
Childhood Education, City College of New York

Photography

Herbert Seignoret
Mathematics in the City, City College of New York

Illustrator

Susan Havice

Schools featured in photographs

The Muscota New School/PS 314 (an empowerment school in Region 10), New York, NY
Independence School/PS 234 (Region 9), New York, NY
Fort River Elementary School, Amherst, MA

Contents

Unit Overview

This unit begins with the story of a pajama party—a sleepover during which eight children play, moving up and down bunk beds, teasing the babysitter who imagines she is losing and then gaining children! The unit introduces the arithmetic rack as a powerful model and tool to act out the story. The arithmetic rack is a calculating frame consisting of two rows of ten beads with two sets of five in each row. (Instructions for creating or buying your own arithmetic racks are included on page 59.)

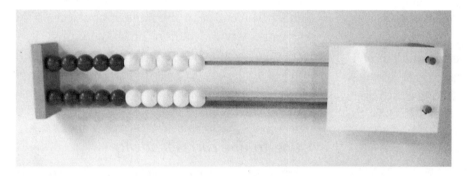

The five-structure of this apparatus supports the development of part-whole relations in early number sense. Since five is a quantity that can often be perceived as a whole, it can be used to support understanding 6 as 5 + 1, or 4 as 5 − 1. It also supports the strategies of doubles and near doubles,

The Landscape of Learning

BIG IDEAS

- ☀ Cardinality
- ☀ One-to-one correspondence
- ☀ Hierarchical inclusion
- ☀ Compensation and equivalence

STRATEGIES

- ☀ Using synchrony and one-to-one tagging (vs. double or skip-tagging)
- ☀ Counting three times and counting on
- ☀ Using trial and error vs. systematic production of arrangements

MODEL

- ☀ Arithmetic rack

$6 + 7 = 6 + 6 + 1$, and making tens, $9 + 6 = 10 + 5$. In this unit, children move the beads on the arithmetic rack to illustrate and develop an understanding that eight can be named in many ways, for example as $7 + 1$, $5 + 3$, or $4 + 4$. The unit also includes the game Up and Down the Ladder, and employs the use of quick images (a series of related problems flashed only for seconds) to further develop early number sense.

As the unit progresses, the context shifts to an exploration of apple boxes. Children investigate the number of unique combinations for five apples of two kinds, green and red, and record the combinations for a grocer who is confused about how many arrangements there can be. In contrast to the bunk beds investigation in which children can easily imagine someone going up and down the ladder, now they must exchange. That is, instead of moving a counter to another group, the counter must be removed and replaced. This action is more difficult. The recording sheet for the grocer is designed in such a way that a staircase pattern emerges as one red apple is traded for a green apple each time. Boxes holding various numbers of apples (such as six, seven, eight, nine, and ten) are then explored to examine if the staircase pattern will always occur. Data are also collected on the number of possible arrangements for each box: A box of six apples has five possible arrangements; a box of seven has six arrangements; a box of ten has nine arrangements. This supports the development of a systematic way of producing all the possible arrangements and produces another inquiry: Can we predict the number of arrangements if we know the size of the box?

The unit ends with the Part-Whole Bingo game. This game can be played throughout the year as a way for children to extend composing and decomposing strategies as they establish equivalence, for example representing 7 as $5 + 2$ or as $3 + 4$, or even as $2 + 2 + 2 + 1$.

The Mathematical Landscape

The mathematical focus of this unit is early number sense. On the landscape of learning for early number sense there are several big ideas, strategies, and models. These have been researched extensively (Piaget 1965; Gravemeijer 1994; Kamii 1985; Treffers 1991). Each is described in the section that follows.

BIG IDEAS

This unit is designed to encourage the development of:

❖ **cardinality**

❖ **one-to-one correspondence**

❖ **hierarchical inclusion**

❖ **compensation and equivalence**

❖ Cardinality

Young children often count by rote first, before they count with meaning. Counting with meaning requires an understanding of the purpose of counting, an understanding of cardinality—that the number they end on is the number of objects in the set. Thus, when children finish counting, it is important to ask, "So how many do you have?" Don't assume that because they seem to count well they understand that 8 means eight objects. They may think the eighth object is 8.

❖ One-to-one correspondence

Children also need to construct the big idea of one-to-one correspondence—that if there is a corresponding object matched to each object in a set, the sets are equivalent. For example, if there are eight children at a sleepover party, eight cups and eight napkins are needed so that everyone will get one of each.

❖ Hierarchical inclusion

Even when children do understand cardinality and one-to-one correspondence, they still may not realize that the numbers grow by one, and exactly one, each time. Researchers call this idea hierarchical inclusion (Kamii 1985). They mean that amounts nest inside each other: six includes five, plus one; five includes four, plus one, etc.

❖ Compensation and equivalence

Children may initially have a difficult time comprehending that $5 + 3$ is equivalent to $4 + 4$. The big ideas here are compensation and equivalence—that if you lose one (from the five, for example) but gain it (onto the three), the total stays the same.

STRATEGIES

As you work with the activities in this unit, you will notice that children use many strategies to derive number combinations. Here are some strategies to notice:

❖ *using synchrony and one-to-one tagging*

❖ *counting three times vs. counting on*

❖ *using trial and error vs. systematic production of arrangements*

❖ Using synchrony and one-to-one tagging

Counting effectively requires children to coordinate many actions simultaneously. Not only must they remember the word that comes next, they must use only one word for each object (synchrony) and tag each object once and only once (one-to-one tagging). Initially when children are learning to count, this coordination is very difficult; they often skip some objects, double tag others, and are not synchronized, using too many or too few words for the number of objects they are counting.

❖ Counting three times vs. counting on

Making groups and determining the total number of objects in all the groups is also a huge undertaking. To determine the whole when adding the objects in two groups, children may tediously count three times—first each of the two groups and then the whole, starting from one each time. For example, to determine if 6 red apples and 4 green apples complete a box of 10 apples, they may count 1 through 6, 1 through 4, and then 1 through 10. They may even make wrong sets and then start all over again with a new trial when the first doesn't work, rather than fixing it to work. A major landmark strategy to notice and celebrate is when a child begins to count on—labeling the first set 6 and then continuing "7, 8, 9, 10, so 4 greens!"

❖ Using trial and error vs. systematic production of arrangements

Often children begin to make arrangements using trial and error. Once they construct the big ideas of compensation and equivalence (i.e., that 5 + 3 = 4 + 4)

and hierarchical inclusion (that numbers nest inside each other and grow by one each time), a major change in strategy may occur as they use these ideas to generate all the possibilities systematically— turning 9 + 1 into 8 + 2, then 7 + 3, etc.

MATHEMATICAL MODELING

The model introduced in this unit is the arithmetic rack (the Dutch term is *rekenrek*) developed by Adri Treffers, a researcher at the Freudenthal Institute in the Netherlands. Based on much developmental research, the arithmetic rack was designed to align with children's early number sense strategies, enabling them to move from counting one by one to decomposing and composing numbers with subunits (Treffers 1991).

Models go through three stages of development (Gravemeijer 1999; Fosnot and Dolk 2001):

❖ *model of the situation*

❖ *model of children's strategies*

❖ *model as a tool for thinking*

❖ Model of the situation

The arithmetic rack model supports children in their attempts to envision the part-whole relations of number with five as a special unit. The rack's features—two colors, two rows, and beads that slide—allow children to initially model the situation of children moving up and down the bunk beds.

❖ Model of children's strategies

Children benefit from seeing the teacher model their strategies. Once the model has been introduced as a representation of the situation, you can use it to model the children's strategies as they determine arrangements. If a child counts by ones, move one bead at a time; if a child counts on, move the set, then move beads one at a time onto the set. If a child uses compensation, remove a bead from one group and slide another bead onto the other group.

❖ Model as a tool for thinking

Eventually children will be able to use this model as a tool for thinking—they will be able to imagine 6 + 4 reconfigured as 5 + 5 on the rack. Although not the purpose of this unit, over time the arithmetic rack can become an important model to support children in learning the basic facts for addition and subtraction (Treffers 1991).

Many opportunities to discuss these landmarks in mathematical development will arise as you work through the unit. Look for moments of puzzlement. Don't hesitate to let children discuss their ideas and check and recheck their counting. Celebrate their accomplishments just as you would a toddler's first steps when learning to walk.

A graphic of the full landscape of learning for early number sense, addition, and subtraction is provided on page 9. The purpose of this graphic is to allow you to see the longer journey of children's mathematical development and to place your work with this unit within the scope of this long-term development. You may also find it helpful to use this graphic as a way to record the progress of individual children for yourself. Each landmark can be shaded in as you find evidence in a child's work and in what the child says—evidence that a big idea, landmark strategy, or way of modeling has been constructed. In a sense, you will be recording the individual pathways children take as they develop as young mathematicians.

References and Resources

Dolk, Maarten and Catherine Twomey Fosnot. 2004a. *Addition and Subtraction Minilessons, Grades PreK–3.* CD-ROM with accompanying facilitator's guide by Antonia Cameron, Sherrin B. Hersch and Catherine Twomey Fosnot. Portsmouth, NH: Heinemann.

———. 2004b. *Fostering Children's Mathematical Development, Grades PreK–3: The Landscape of Learning.* CD-ROM with accompanying facilitator's guide by Sherrin B. Hersch, Antonia Cameron and Catherine Twomey Fosnot. Portsmouth, NH: Heinemann.

Fosnot, Catherine Twomey and Maarten Dolk. 2001. *Young Mathematicians at Work: Constructing Number Sense, Addition, and Subtraction.* Portsmouth, NH: Heinemann.

Gravemeijer, Koeno P. E. 1994. *Developing Realistic Mathematics Education.* Utrecht, Netherlands: Freudenthal Institute.

———. 1999. How emergent models may foster the constitution of formal mathematics. *Mathematical Thinking and Learning, 1*(2), 155–77.

Kamii, Constance. 1985. *Young Children Reinvent Arithmetic.* New York: Teachers College Press.

Piaget, Jean. 1965. *The Child's Conception of Number.* New York: Routledge.

Treffers, Adri. 1991. *Rekenen tot twentig met het rekenrek* [Calculating to twenty with the arithmetic rack]. *Willem Bartjens* 10 (1): 35–45.

NUMBER SENSE, ADDITION, and SUBTRACTION

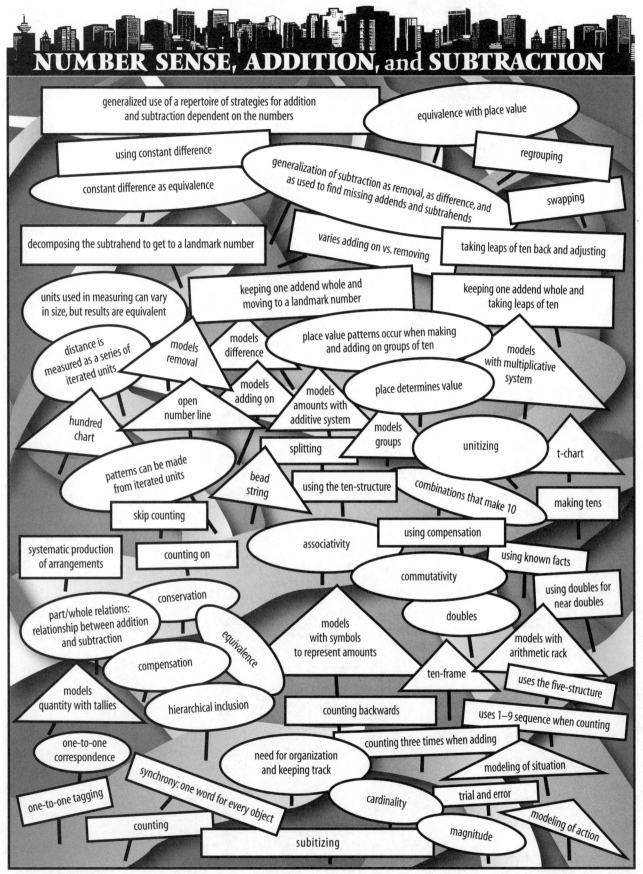

generalized use of a repertoire of strategies for addition and subtraction dependent on the numbers

equivalence with place value

using constant difference

regrouping

constant difference as equivalence

generalization of subtraction as removal, as difference, and as used to find missing addends and subtrahends

swapping

decomposing the subtrahend to get to a landmark number

varies adding on vs. removing

taking leaps of ten back and adjusting

units used in measuring can vary in size, but results are equivalent

keeping one addend whole and moving to a landmark number

keeping one addend whole and taking leaps of ten

distance is measured as a series of iterated units

models removal

models difference

place value patterns occur when making and adding on groups of ten

models with multiplicative system

hundred chart

open number line

models adding on

models amounts with additive system

place determines value

models groups

unitizing

t-chart

patterns can be made from iterated units

bead string

splitting

using the ten-structure

combinations that make 10

making tens

skip counting

systematic production of arrangements

counting on

associativity

using compensation

using known facts

commutativity

using doubles for near doubles

conservation

part/whole relations: relationship between addition and subtraction

equivalence

compensation

doubles

models with symbols to represent amounts

models with arithmetic rack

models quantity with tallies

hierarchical inclusion

ten-frame

uses the five-structure

counting backwards

uses 1–9 sequence when counting

one-to-one correspondence

need for organization and keeping track

counting three times when adding

modeling of situation

one-to-one tagging

synchrony: one word for every object

cardinality

trial and error

modeling of action

counting

magnitude

subitizing

The landscape of learning: number sense, addition, and subtraction on the horizon showing landmark strategies (rectangles), big ideas (ovals), and models (triangles).

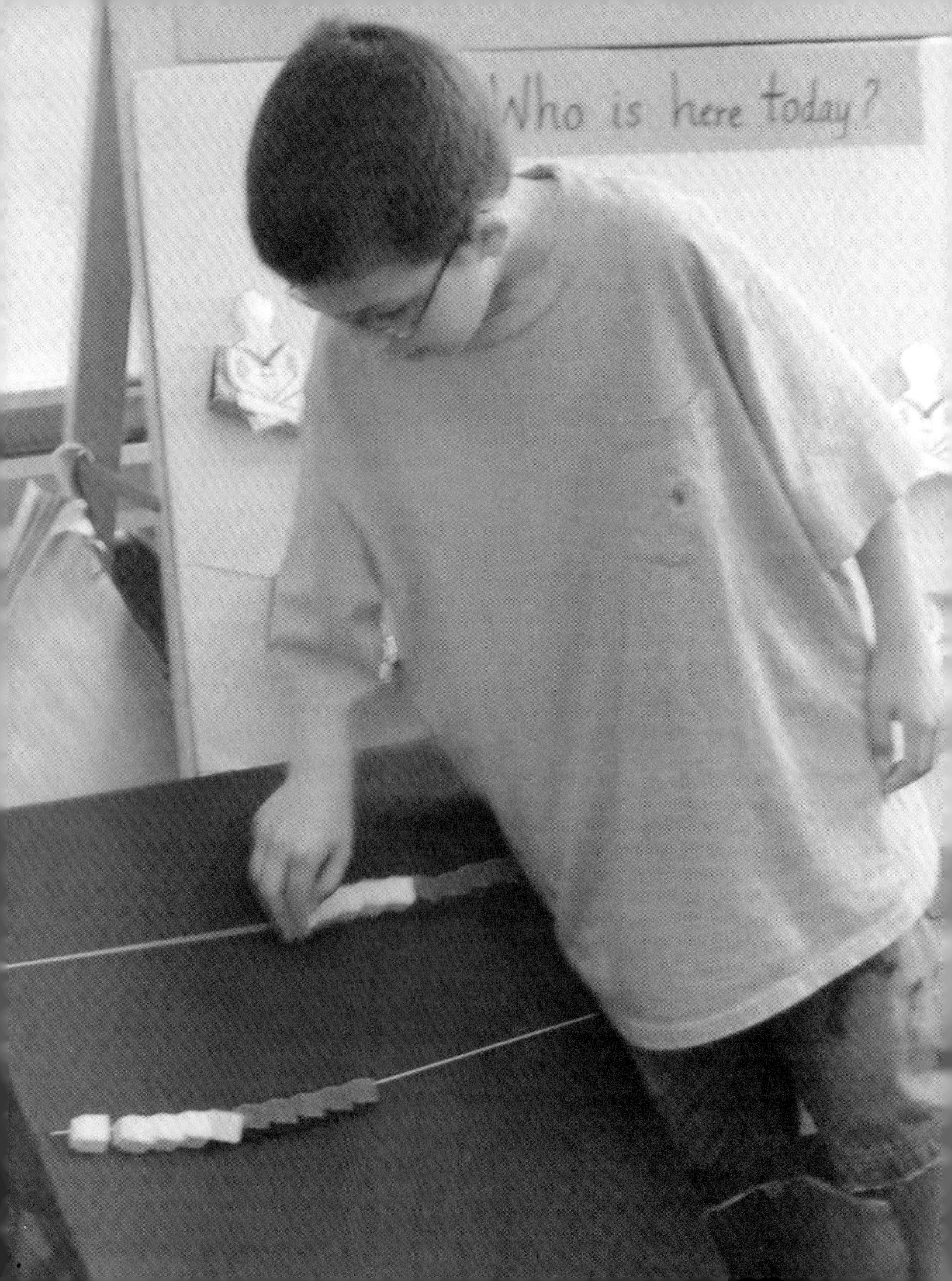
Who is here today?

Bunk Beds

The story of *The Sleepover* sets the stage for investigating various arrangements of eight people on bunk beds. After the children hear the story and act it out, they go off to investigate, find, and record various arrangements. The arithmetic rack and the bunk bed context are introduced and used to support the development of compensation and equivalence; for example, five on the top bunk and three on the bottom are explored as being equivalent to four on the top and four on the bottom.

Day One Outline

Developing the Context

☀ Read and discuss *The Sleepover*.

☀ Help children act out the story using the arithmetic rack.

Supporting the Investigation

☀ Note children's strategies as they explore different ways to arrange eight children on bunk beds.

Materials Needed

The Sleepover [If you do not have the full-color read-aloud book (available from Heinemann), you can use Appendix A.]

Class-size arithmetic rack, with cover-up board or cloth

Individual arithmetic rack—one per pair of children

Instructions for making both types of arithmetic racks can be found in Appendix B. Visit contextsforlearning.com for information on where to purchase arithmetic racks.

Student recording sheet for the arithmetic rack investigation (Appendix C)—two per child

Attendance strips *(optional)* **(Appendix D)**

Large chart pad and easel (or chalkboard or whiteboard)

Markers

Developing the Context

☀ Read and discuss *The Sleepover*.

☀ Help children act out the story using the arithmetic rack.

Read *The Sleepover* (Appendix A). Allow children to discuss their ideas about whether Aunt Kate has enough napkins and if there are other ways the children in the story can trick her. Encourage them to discuss how it was that 5 + 3 cups of juice was just the right amount for 6 + 2 children. Have the children act out the story using the class-size arithmetic rack:

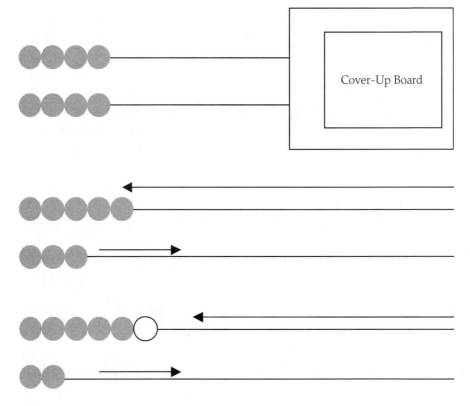

Record the result as 4 + 4 = 5 + 3 = 6 + 2.

Developing the Context

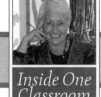
Sarah: One, 2, 3, 4, 5, 6, 7, 8! It's still 8!

Megan: Four on the top and 4 on the bottom make 8, and 5 and 3 are 8!

Caroline: Let me check. That's 3 on the bottom, 4, 5, 6, 7, 8! It is still 8!

Anna *(the teacher)*: So there are still 8 kids? $4 + 4 = 5 + 3$? Is that true?

Patti: One kid just went up the ladder!

Anna: Oh…look at that! You think maybe a kid went up the ladder? So one kid more on the top and one less now on the bottom bunk? *(Writes:)*

$$4 + 4 = 5 + 3$$

Author's Notes

Many children will need to count to check and will count by ones. Some children may miss a bead or count some beads twice. If this happens, have the children help each other and double-check. Other children may be able to see small amounts as units and will then count on. Some children may know the facts, but still not be able to explain what happened.

The big idea to focus on is compensation. One is lost, but then one is gained, so the total stays the same. Help children realize this by staying in the context of the bunk beds and discussing how one person must have gone up the ladder. It is not expected at this point that children will have systematic ways to determine all of the combinations.

Anna symbolizes equivalence by writing an equation. Many children think the equal sign means "the answer is coming." By writing equivalent expressions and using the equal sign (e.g. $4 + 4 = 5 + 3$) you can prevent this misconception from developing.

Supporting the Investigation

Pass out the recording sheets (Appendix C) and suggest that children work at tables with partners to find as many ways as they can to arrange the eight children on the bunk beds. Have them record the arrangements they find. Provide them with individual arithmetic racks. As children work, walk around and take note of the strategies you see. Have children put their recording sheets in their work folders when they are done.

☀ Note children's strategies as they explore different ways to arrange eight children on bunk beds.

■ Assessment Tips

Note which children need to count to be certain that the total is still the same. Note their counting strategies, such as whether they are counting each bead or skipping some. Note which children know without needing to count. It is helpful to jot down your observations on sticky notes. Later, you can place these on the children's recording sheets to be included in their portfolios.

Sample Children's Work

In Figure 1, one-to-one correspondence and cardinality are not yet evident. Several children have been drawn on the bunk beds but all are random amounts.

Figure 2 does show one-to-one correspondence with a total of eight children. Some arrangements have been found, but some are duplicates and there is no systematic approach to finding all the arrangements.

In Figure 3, the duplicates have been crossed out, although all the combinations still have not been found.

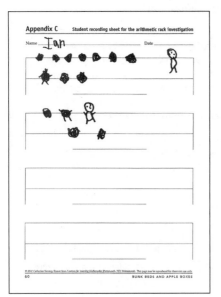

Figure 1

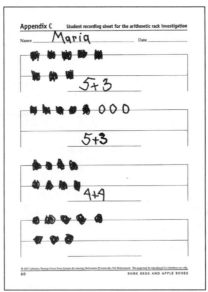

Figure 2

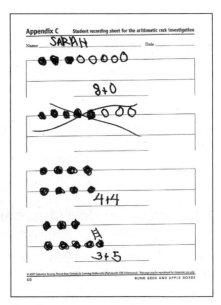

Figure 3

Differentiating Instruction

Some children may find it difficult to use the arithmetic rack to represent the children on the bunk beds and to represent the results with a drawing. Suggest that they use the attendance strips instead as it may be easier for them to model the situation more concretely by actually moving the paper cutouts up and down. (See Appendix D.)

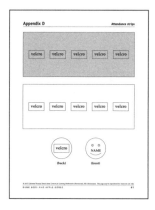

Reflections on the Day

Today, children were introduced to the context of bunk beds and they came up with several strategies for finding arrangements of eight. You were able to witness the variety of strategies and to see who is still struggling with one-to-one correspondence and counting. You also had the opportunity to support the development of equivalence and compensation. On Day Two, children will continue with this work and you will have a math congress to discuss a few of these strategies.

Day One   15

DAY TWO
Bunk Beds

Children return to work to review the combinations they found on Day One and to add any more they can think of. The purpose of revisiting this context is to allow for reflection on and revision to children's previous drafts. After they reflect and revise their work, they will discuss their work in a math congress.

Day Two Outline

Preparing for the Math Congress

☀ As children review their work from Day One, determine who will share during the congress.

Facilitating the Math Congress

☀ Record the arrangements children have found.

☀ Use the arithmetic rack to explore the arrangements and model children's strategies.

Preparing for the Math Congress

Remind children of the bunk bed story and their investigation on Day One. Have them get their recording sheets from their work folders and with their partners review and reflect on all the ways they found to arrange the children on the bunk beds. Have new recording sheets available (Appendix C) in case they want to add combinations they had not thought of before. Ask children to reflect on the following questions:

✦ Are any of the arrangements the same?

✦ How do they know they have them all?

✦ Is there a strategy they found helpful?

☀ As children review their work from Day One, determine who will share during the congress.

Tips for Structuring the Math Congress

As the children prepare, think about how you will structure the congress. You might find it useful to scaffold this conversation from children's struggles toward strategies that helped. To determine which children will share during the congress, observe them as they work, looking for those who

✦ do not show evidence of one-to-one correspondence: they have drawn too many children on the recording sheet.

✦ have figured out a way to produce one combination from another or a way to keep track, even if they have found only a few combinations.

✦ are attempting a systematic approach. It is not likely that children at this point will produce all the combinations systematically, but any movement toward a systematic approach is important to discuss.

Facilitating the Math Congress

Convene the children in the meeting area to discuss the combinations they found. Have them sit next to their partners with their recording sheets. Have the children you have chosen share their combinations and make a list on a large chart of the combinations as they do so. You can also use the class-size arithmetic rack to check out some of the combinations and to model their strategies.

☀ Record the arrangements children have found.

☀ Use the arithmetic rack to explore the arrangements and model children's strategies.

Anna *(the teacher):* Ian, come tell us about what you did. *(Ian comes to the front of the group and holds up his work for all to see).*

Ian: I drew pictures of the kids on the bunk beds.

Anna: You did. And they are beautiful pictures, too! It was hard to keep track of how many to draw, wasn't it? How many of you found it hard to keep track, too? *(Several kids raise hands.)* Let's check out one together. *(Anna moves four beads as a group on the top of the class arithmetic rack and invites Ian to check out how many.)* Check me, Ian. How many do we have so far?

Ian: 1, 2, 3, 4.

Anna: How many?

Ian: 4.

Anna: How many shall we put on the bottom bunk? We need to have 8 kids altogether, right?

Ian: 3. *(He holds up three fingers.)*

Anna: Let's see if that is enough. *(Moves three beads.)* I wonder how many we have now?

Ian: 1, 2, 3, 4, 5, 6, 7…it's not enough. *(He pushes over another bead.)*

Anna: Wow. Four on the top and 4 on the bottom. There's a new arrangement to add to your sheet. *(Ian beams.)* I wonder if we could use this arrangement to make another. You have a strategy you used that might help us here, Sarah. Would you share next?

Sarah: I used one that worked and made a kid go down the ladder. Like this. *(She pushes one bead away and adds another to the bottom, ending with 3 and 5.)*

Anna: Turn to the person you are sitting next to and talk about what Sarah did. Will this strategy always work?

Author's Notes

By starting with Ian's struggle to keep track of the quantity, Anna invites the children in the congress to consider helpful ways to proceed besides trial and error and counting.

Ian does not subitize the four as a unit. He needs to count them. Anna does not supply Ian with an answer but checks to see if he realizes that the number he ends on when counting is the amount of the group—cardinality.

Anna accepts his answer but supports him to reflect on it.

Ian's strategy is to count the total by ones. He does not count on. He does know that by adding one more he can turn seven into eight—hierarchical inclusion.

Sarah's strategy of moving one might extend and support Ian's development, as well as the development of other children. By having Sarah share next, Anna pushes the community to consider compensation.

By asking the children for pair talk, Anna engages all the children in considering the strategy and pushes the children to explain and generalize about what is happening.

Reflections on the Day

Today, children had the opportunity to monitor and reflect on their thinking by reviewing and revising their work. They reflected on the following questions: Do I have all possible combinations? How do I know? Do I have duplicates? What is my strategy? In the congress, they were encouraged to consider ways to work more systematically by making one arrangement into another, to keep track, and to use strategies such as compensation to make equivalent expressions.

DAY THREE
Bunk Beds

Materials Needed

Class-size arithmetic rack, with cover-up board

Individual arithmetic rack—one per child

Drawing paper—a few sheets per child

Markers

Quick images with the arithmetic rack are used to support the use of the five-structure in determining "how many?" The quick images also provide the context for a narrative structure. After each quick image children discuss what most likely happened: did someone go down the ladder; and/or did someone leave the room and return later? For the remainder of math workshop, children will write their own sleepover stories. They will choose a different number and tell a story about the changing combinations.

Day Three Outline

Developing the Context

☀ Use the arithmetic rack to present quick images designed to support the development of compensation.

Supporting the Investigation

☀ Help children create and share their own sleepover stories.

Developing the Context

Use the class-size arithmetic rack to flash various quick images of different arrangements. Show the arrangement for only a few seconds, and then place the cover-up board over the image. (If you prefer, you can use a piece of fabric to cover the image after it is shown.) Each time you show an image, ask, "How many kids (beads) are at the bunk bed party?" and "How do you know?" Also ask, "What happened on the beds?" "Did anyone go up or down the ladder? Leave the room? Come back?" etc.

Suggested arrangements include:

- Five on the top, three on the bottom
- Four on the top, four on the bottom
- Four on the top, three on the bottom
- Three on the top, five on the bottom
- Two on the top, six on the bottom
- Eight on the bottom

☀ Use the arithmetic rack to present quick images designed to support the development of compensation.

Behind the Numbers

The numbers for the quick images have been chosen carefully to support the development of compensation. The five and three from the first image becomes four and four. One has gone down the ladder. The third problem uses a total of seven, not eight. This is purposeful. Encourage children to think about what happened. Did someone leave the room? The fourth problem uses eight again and this time one from the top bunk has moved to the bottom. Did the person who left also return? Support children to describe the change from one image to the next.

Supporting the Investigation

After discussion, give children drawing paper. Suggest they choose a number and make their own sleepover stories. Have them use their own individual arithmetic racks as they work. Help children choose numbers for their stories that they can handle. Five is a suitable number for children who are struggling because they may see small amounts like three and two as a whole without having to count (subitizing). Other children may be able to handle much larger numbers.

☀ Help children create and share their own sleepover stories.

When children have had a sufficient amount of time to create their stories, ask them to choose partners. Have partners read their stories to each other and discuss them. Or, if you prefer, bring the children to the meeting area and have a few children read their stories aloud to the whole group. As stories are read, use the class-size arithmetic rack to model the changing arrangements.

Literacy Connection

Children's sleepover stories can be revised and edited and brought to the publication stage. They can be bound and placed in the classroom library, just as you would do when children write stories during writing workshop. This publication allows children to revisit the mathematics over and over throughout the year, as they enjoy reading and rereading each other's stories.

Reflections on the Day

Today, by using the arithmetic rack for quick images, children were provided with opportunities to make use of the five-structure in determining amounts. Four is one less than five; six is one more than five. They were asked to mentally compose and decompose numbers and examine and explain what might have happened when the arrangements changed. The quick image activity served as a context for developing narratives as children wrote their own mathematics stories. Instead of a math congress, children spent group time reading their stories aloud.

DAY FOUR
Bunk Beds

Today, the context for learning is a new game, Up and Down the Ladder. After you introduce the game and model how to play, children play the game in pairs. The game supports the development of equations as children find equivalent arrangements. Further opportunities to investigate compensation and equivalence are also provided.

Day Four Outline

Developing the Context

☀ Model how to play Up and Down the Ladder.

Supporting the Investigation

☀ Note children's strategies as they play the game.

Materials Needed

Student recording sheet for Up and Down the Ladder (Appendix E)—one per child

Up and Down the Ladder game cards (Appendix F)—one set per pair of children

Number cubes (with dots, one through six)—two per pair of children

Plastic teddy bears (or other counters such as cubes)—twelve per pair of children

Markers

Developing the Context

☀ Model how to play Up and Down the Ladder.

Bring the children to a meeting area and have them sit in a circle. Play Up and Down the Ladder with one child in the center of the circle as a way to introduce the game to the class and model how the game is played.

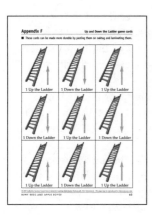

■ Object of the Game

This game is designed to provide children with experiences in moving pieces up and down the ladder, compensating while maintaining equivalence. It also provides them with a realistic context to write equations.

■ Directions for Playing Up and Down the Ladder

Children play the game in pairs and take turns rolling a pair of number cubes.

The roll on each number cube determines the number of teddy bears on the bunk beds. For example, if a 5 and a 2 are rolled, Player One takes seven teddy bears and places five of them on the top line and two of them on the bottom line of the recording sheet (Appendix E). On the line below, Player One writes 5 + 2 and then colors five circles on the top and two on the bottom in place of the seven teddy bears.

Player Two then picks an Up and Down the Ladder game card (Appendix F) and rearranges the seven teddy bears on the bunk bed to the right according to the card's instructions. For example, if the card says "1 Up the Ladder," Player Two removes one bear from the bottom and places it on the top. Player Two then records 6 + 1 and colors six circles on the top and one on the bottom.

Player Two then rolls the number cubes and play continues as above until both players' recording sheets are completed. *[See Figure 4]*

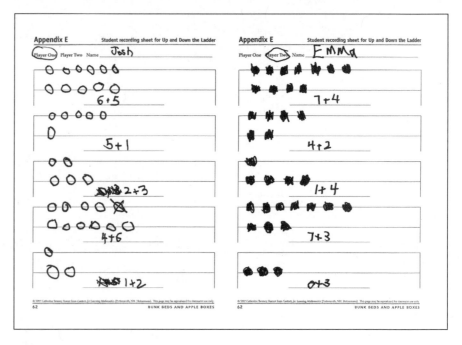

Figure 4

Supporting the Investigation

Assign partners and have the children go to tables to play. Give each child a recording sheet and give each pair of children a dozen counters, a pair of number cubes, and a pack of cards. On the top of each recording sheet, players should circle whether they are Player One or Player Two.

☀ Note children's strategies as they play the game.

■ Assessment Tips

As you walk around supporting children as they play the game, take note of which children need to count to be certain that the total is still the same. Also note their counting strategies, such as whether they are counting each dot on the number cubes or skipping some, or whether they can subitize the amount on each number cube and know without needing to count. When determining the changed result, note whether they count each group and the total, thereby counting three times, or whether they know the result without counting. It is helpful to jot down your observations on sticky notes. Later, you can place these on the children's recording sheets to be included in their portfolios.

Reflections on the Day

Today, children had opportunities within the context of a game to revisit arranging parts to make a whole, rearranging by removing from one part and adding to the other part while maintaining equivalence, and writing equivalent expressions.

Apple Boxes

Materials Needed

Apple boxes picture (Appendix G)

Before class, prepare a copy (or transparency) of Appendix G. Color the apples in one box red and the apples in the other box green.

Student recording sheet for the apple boxes investigation (Appendix H)—one per child, with extras available

Red and green connecting cubes— one small bin per pair of children, as needed

Red and green markers

Large chart pad and easel

A new context, apple boxes, is introduced with the story of a grocer who wants to sell boxes containing both green and red apples. Children are asked to consider all the combinations for two kinds of apples, with five in a box. After investigating and recording all possible combinations, a math congress is convened to discuss and ensure that quantity, not arrangement, is the focus. Duplicate arrangements are eliminated.

Day Five Outline

Developing the Context

☀ Use pictures to introduce the apple boxes investigation.

Supporting the Investigation

☀ Support children as they explore different ways to combine green and red apples in a box of five.

Preparing for the Math Congress

☀ Plan a congress to highlight duplicate vs. unique arrangements.

Facilitating the Math Congress

☀ As children share, discuss which combinations are duplicates.

☀ Record a list of unique combinations and calculate the total number of possible combinations.

Developing the Context

Tell children you went to the grocery store the other day and noticed that the grocer had boxes of apples like those in the pictures. (Show children the two boxes in Appendix G.) Some boxes had only red apples; other boxes had only green apples. Encourage the children to figure out with you how many apples are in each box.

Explain that you wanted some of both kinds of apples but you didn't want to buy two boxes. So you asked the grocer why he didn't have one box that was mixed, with *some* green and *some* red. The grocer said that he had intended to make some boxes like that, but the many different ways to combine the apples confused him. For example, if he just put one red apple in the box, he wasn't sure how many green he would need. Encourage the children to figure out with you that four green apples would be needed to fill the box.

Suggest that since they have already been exploring bunk bed combinations and know a lot about making different arrangements, you thought they could help the grocer by creating some pictures of the different apple combinations he might make.

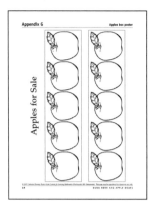

☀ Use pictures to introduce the apple boxes investigation.

Supporting the Investigation

Assign partners and pass out recording sheets (Appendix H) to each pair of children. Suggest that they work together at tables, using drawings or connecting cubes, to find as many ways as they can to arrange green and red apples in boxes of five. Have extra copies of the recording sheets available so that children can make as many combinations as they can think of. Have them color the apples in the boxes with red and green markers or crayons. Have children work on this investigation for about twenty minutes, while you walk around and support their work.

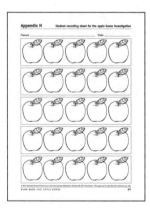

☀ Support children as they explore different ways to combine green and red apples in a box of five.

Preparing for the Math Congress

Before bringing the children back together for a math congress to discuss their findings, note whether some of them have made duplicate boxes. For example, many children think that a box that is arranged red, green, red, green, red is a different box than red, red, red, green, green. You will want to use the math congress to establish the idea that although the arrangements may not look alike, the numbers of green and red apples are equivalent. Be prepared to use the context to help children realize that only the numbers matter by reminding them that customers care only about *how many* red and green apples they are getting, not how the apples are arranged.

☀ Plan a congress to highlight duplicate vs. unique arrangements.

◼ Tips for Structuring the Math Congress

Look for children who have duplicates:

✦ Who have confused arrangement with quantity *[See Figure 5]*

✦ Who have pictures that are identical *[See Figure 6]*

Figure 5

Figure 6

Facilitating the Math Congress

☀ As children share, discuss which combinations are duplicates.

☀ Record a list of unique combinations and calculate the total number of possible combinations.

Convene the children in the meeting area to discuss the combinations they found. Have them sit next to their partners with their recording sheets. Start by having two or three children share the strategies they found helpful. Ask children to consider boxes of apples that have different combinations, but equivalent amounts. Remind children that customers care only about how many of each kind of apple they get, not how the apples are arranged, because once they take the apples out of the box they just have a pile of apples anyway. Help children move the connecting cubes to establish which arrangements are duplicates. Then have the children share their combinations while you make a list of the unique arrangements on large chart paper. Write the total number of combinations on it, i.e., The box of five had four possible combinations. Keep this chart because you will refer back to it on Day Six.

A Portion of the Math Congress

Anna *(the teacher)*: Some of you made a box that looked like this: red, red, red, green, green. And some of you made a box like this: green, green, red, red, red. *(Anna lays out two boxes and places cubes on them to make arrangements.)* I'm wondering if these are really different plans. What do you think? Talk to the person next to you about this. *(Pair talk.)* Jaleelah, start us off. What did you and Juan talk about?

Jaleelah: Those two boxes are the same. You can just turn one.

Anna: Come show us what you mean. *(Jaleelah turns one box 180 degrees.)*

Several kids: Oh…they are the same.

Jaleelah: And the customer could just turn it.

Anna: What about this one: red, green, red, green, red. Does this have the same amounts, too?

Colleen: I think it is still the same, 'cause you could just move them.

Peter: And the customer is still getting 3 red and 2 green.

Anna: And that is all the customer cares about, right? How many, not what they look like. And there are still 3 red and 2 green in all of these? *(Establishes agreement.)* Let's just count 3 red and 2 green as one box then, and let's make a list of what we have so far. Did anyone find a way with just one red? How many green were needed?

Author's Notes

By starting with the children's struggles, Anna invites them to consider equivalence.

Anna provides pair talk as a way to get everyone engaged in thinking.

Anna invites the community to discuss and prove their ideas to each other.

Having established equivalence by using the context and focusing on quantity rather than arrangement, Anna can now generate with the class the list of unique boxes. Four boxes are listed in order: 1 red + 4 green; 2 red + 3 green; 3 red + 2 green; 4 red + 1 green. The total number of combinations is also recorded.

Reflections on the Day

Today children were provided with another opportunity to build equivalent arrangements. In the prior bunk bed context, children could imagine someone physically going up and down the ladder, and the arithmetic rack was provided as a support. In the apple box context, a red apple needed to be *exchanged* for a green apple, a slightly more difficult action for young children to imagine.

Apple Boxes

Today children begin to work with the ten-structure, making all possible combinations of ten apples in two colors. After investigating, a math congress is held—this time it is structured in a way to produce a visual image of a staircase representing all the possible combinations. Children are encouraged to wonder if this pattern will appear for any number and to generalize.

Day Six Outline

Developing the Context

☀ Explain that the grocer now wants to make a box of green and red apples twice as big—a box of ten.

Supporting the Investigation

☀ Note children's strategies as they search for all combinations.

☀ Challenge children to keep track so they can identify every combination.

Facilitating the Math Congress

☀ Systematically record the unique combinations on graph paper.

☀ Encourage children to reflect on the pattern that appears.

☀ Make a class big book entitled *The Big Box of Ten!*

Developing the Context

Explain that the grocer was so pleased with what the children had done on Day Five that he decided to make a box twice as big—a big box of ten apples.

☀ Explain that the grocer now wants to make a box of green and red apples twice as big—a box of ten.

Supporting the Investigation

Assign pairs to work together just as on Day Five (this time, however, children should use the recording sheet found in Appendix I). Move around the room, helping children find combinations and reminding them that customers care only about the numbers of the apples, not about how they are arranged. Challenge them to find a way to keep track so that they are sure they have found every possible combination.

☀ Note children's strategies as they search for all combinations.

☀ Challenge children to keep track so they can identify every combination.

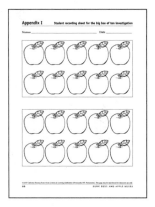

▨ Assessment Tips

Note which children still need to count to be sure if the total is still the same. Note their counting strategies. Are any children counting on, rather than three times? Note specifically whether more children are beginning to approach the problem systematically by using compensation—systematically removing one each time. It is helpful to jot down your observations on sticky notes. Later, you can place these on the children's recording sheets to be included in their portfolios. Make special note of children's developmental progress.

Facilitating the Math Congress

Rather than having individual children share their strategies in this congress, use the graph paper to structure the recording of the results.

Ask if anyone found a way to make a box with just one green apple, and if so how many reds were needed? Then ask about two green, then three green, etc. Explain that you are not drawing the boxes, but making a recording of the *exact* numbers of red and green apples to be sure you have

☀ Systematically record the unique combinations on graph paper.

☀ Encourage children to reflect on the pattern that appears.

☀ Make a class big book entitled *The Big Box of Ten!*

all the ways they could be arranged. Systematically record the class findings on the graph paper, as shown below:

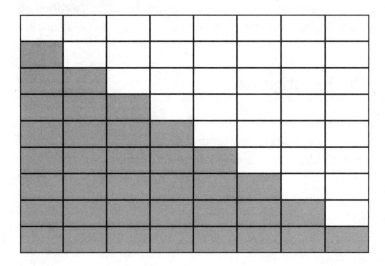

Let the children be surprised that a staircase results and marvel with them. Wonder with them if this staircase happened only because there were ten in a box. Ask: "Will this always happen?" Note with them that there were nine possible arrangements for the big box of ten and four for the box of five. Ask: "Do you think there might be eleven ways for a box of twelve?" Encourage them to think about why.

Literacy Connection

Make your own class big book, *The Big Box of Ten!* Narrate and type up the story of what your class did as they worked on the big box investigation. Include several samples of the children's work and end the book with the class chart and the question about the staircase: Will this always happen? You will use this big book on Day Seven to develop the context for a continuing investigation.

Reflections on the Day

The math congress today helped to tighten the focus on the pattern of the exchange, one green for one red, and the resulting pattern of all possible combinations as a staircase. It also pushed the children to consider other situations and to *generalize* about the relations and number of combinations that are possible for any given box.

DAY SEVEN
Apple Boxes

The class big book created on Day Six is used today as a context to open up the apple boxes inquiry into an exploration of many different size boxes. The purpose is to continue to promote generalization and working systematically, exchanging one apple for another each time. Children are also challenged to predict how many combinations there will be for any given size box.

Day Seven Outline

Developing the Context

☀ Read *The Big Box of Ten!*

Supporting the Investigation

☀ Note children's strategies as they investigate combinations for other sizes of apple boxes.

☀ Encourage children to reflect on and generalize the patterns that result.

Materials Needed

The Big Box of Ten! book from Day Six

Red and green connecting cubes— one small bin per pair of children, as needed

Drawing paper—a few sheets per pair of children

Red and green markers

Developing the Context

☀ Read *The Big Box of Ten!*

Read the class big book, *The Big Box of Ten!,* from Day Six.

Supporting the Investigation

☀ Note children's strategies as they investigate combinations for other sizes of apple boxes.

☀ Encourage children to reflect on and generalize the patterns that result.

Encourage the children to investigate other sizes of apple boxes, such as six, seven, eight, nine, twelve, and even fifty! Differentiate your instruction by choosing appropriate numbers for each pair of children. The children again work with partners to explore these boxes and seek all of the unique arrangements. As you walk around the room, share your excitement over children's discussion of the staircase. Wonder with them: "Will this always happen?" Can they anticipate how many combinations there will be? Try to support puzzlement and get them intrigued. Challenge them to think about the bunk beds and how one kid was going up the ladder. Is there a connection between that and swapping a red apple for a green one?

■ Assessment Tips

Note which children still need to count to be sure if the amount is still the same. Note their counting strategies. Are any children counting on, rather than three times? Note specifically the children who are using compensation—removing one each time systematically. Note whether they are generalizing and inferring that the number of arrangements is always one fewer than the number of apples. Can they explain why? How do they explain the occurrence of the pattern? What is the structure of their argument? It is helpful to jot down your observations on sticky notes. Later, you can place these on the children's recording sheets to be included in their portfolios. Make special note of children's developmental progress.

Differentiating Instruction

You can pick different sizes of boxes to differentiate the investigation. Children who are still struggling might work with small boxes, whereas children who need to be challenged can work with much larger boxes. When challenging, don't hesitate to use very large sizes such as 20, 30, 50, or even 100. Using large numbers will push children with good number sense to generalize.

Reflections on the Day

Today children were really encouraged to be young mathematicians at work. By challenging them to investigate large boxes and to wonder about the patterns occurring, you challenged them to generalize and to justify their thinking. These acts get to the heart of what mathematicians do! Today you began the push from arithmetic to algebra—from calculating to noticing patterns and generalizing.

DAY EIGHT
Apple Boxes

The purpose of today's work is to prepare for the math congress on Day Nine. Using large chart paper, children make posters of their findings from their investigation on Day Seven. Using drawings and numerals, children represent as best they can all the apple combinations they found. The subsequent "gallery walk" gives children a chance to review each other's posters and note their comments and questions.

Day Eight Outline

Preparing for the Math Congress

☀ Help children create posters of the arrangements they investigated on Day Seven.

☀ Conduct a gallery walk to give children time to reflect and comment on each other's posters.

Materials Needed

Red and green connecting cubes— one small bin per pair of children, as needed

Large chart paper—one sheet per pair of children

Red and green markers

Sticky notes—one pad per child

Preparing for the Math Congress

* Help children create posters of the arrangements they investigated on Day Seven.

* Conduct a gallery walk to give children time to reflect and comment on each other's posters.

On Day Nine of this unit, you will be having an extensive math congress. To prepare for this, have the children work with their partners to make posters of all the unique arrangements they found for the boxes they investigated on Day Seven. Have children draw all the arrangements they found and help them explain on their posters what they did. When the posters are ready, lay them out around the room either on tables or taped to the wall. Ask children to walk around and look at each other's work. Give them sticky notes to record questions they have, combinations they think are missing, or comments they want to make. They can place notes on each poster for the authors to consider before the math congress on Day Nine.

Be prepared that some arrangements may still be duplicates and that not all possible arrangements may have been found. By having this gallery walk, you are creating further possibilities for thinking and you are encouraging even these young mathematicians to reflect and comment on written forms of mathematics—something professional mathematicians do all the time.

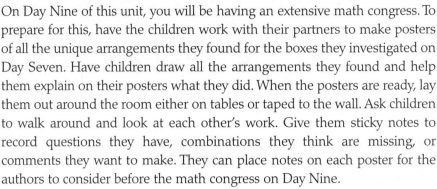

Reflections on the Day

Today you had a chance to really observe the progress your students have made over the course of the past several days. This is a nice moment for you to reflect on the progress of individual children. Understanding equivalence and working systematically to make all possible arrangements using compensation are huge developmental milestones on the journey to developing early number sense.

Even with all the carefully planned investigations in this unit, it is likely that some children are still unable to find all the combinations. That is to be expected. Do not be concerned. Children do not all learn to walk at the same time, either! Even if they cannot find all the combinations, they have probably learned a great deal about number—about quantity—as they participated in these investigations. It is also likely that several children can now anticipate how many combinations there will be for any size box and can proceed systematically to determine them all.

Apple Boxes

Culmination, discussion, and celebration are the focus today as children share their findings in a math congress. Children will revisit the staircase pattern as you record the combinations they found, and this recurring pattern will be discussed at length.

Day Nine Outline

Facilitating the Math Congress

☀ Review the posters created on Day Eight and encourage children to discuss why the staircase pattern keeps appearing.

Materials Needed

Class set of red and green connecting cubes

Easel and chart-size graph paper (with one-inch squares)

Red and green markers

Facilitating the Math Congress

☀ Review the posters created on Day Eight and encourage children to discuss why the staircase pattern keeps appearing.

Convene a math congress to discuss why the staircase pattern is always happening. Record the class solutions onto graph paper systematically, just as you did in the congress on Day Six. Post the results and marvel with the children how the staircase is always appearing. Encourage them to discuss why this is happening.

Inside One Classroom

A Portion of the Math Congress

Anna *(the teacher)*: Let's do the box with 7 apples first. Cassie, you and Leah worked on that one, right? Let's tape your poster up. Tell us what you did and what you found. *(Cassie and Leah tape up poster and turn to the community to share.)*

Cassie: First we found lots of ways, but then we realized that we had already done some of them. So we crossed them out.

Anna: Some kids put some questions and comments on there yesterday, didn't they? Let's see what they say. This one says, "5 + 3 doesn't work." Everybody…turn to the person next to you and decide what you think about this. *(Pair talk.)*

Mike: Doesn't work. It makes 8.

Natasha: It should be 4 + 3.

Anna: Could it be 5 + 2, too? Talk some more about this.

Cassie: It could be both, I think. And 6 + 1. Like the bunk beds. The 2 goes to 1.

Leah: And the 4 goes to 5.

Anna: Hmmm…that's interesting, isn't it? But we don't have a ladder here! *(Laughter.)* Why is this happening? Let's make a recording of Cassie and Leah's work like we did the other day with our big ten box. *(Records on graph paper 1 red and 6 green, 2 red and 5 green, 3 red and 4 green…)*

Several children all together: It's happening again! Look— the staircase!

Anna: Oh my goodness! Why is this happening? Let's look at some other posters and I'll record. We can see if it keeps happening!

continued on next page

Author's Notes

Encourage children to come up and post their posters. Give them a chance to present their strategies and answer questions.

Even when an answer is wrong, the community can work together to consider how to change it. This encourages risk-taking.

Use pair talk as a way to get everyone engaged in thinking and to provide focused reflection time.

Invite children to discuss and prove their ideas to each other. Noticing a pattern is an important beginning, but then mathematicians work to explain why the pattern is happening and if it can be generalized.

continued from previous page

(Two more pairs of children present their work to the community and the teacher records all the possibilities for two more sizes in a structured fashion on the graph paper.)

Several children: It is happening again.

Natasha: It will always happen. It's like each time…a red apple turns green.

Push for generalization. Notice when children use words like always.

Anna: A red becomes green?

Natasha: Yes. First there is only 1 green. Then there are 2, then 3. The greens get more—the reds keep changing to green.

Anna: Who understands what Natasha means? Who can put her idea in different words? Mike?

Asking children to paraphrase each other's ideas encourages them to try to understand and focus on what is being said. Teachers sometimes make the mistake of asking, "Does everyone get that?" Children always nod and the teacher then has no way of knowing whether everyone understands or not. In contrast, when you ask for paraphrasing, you see immediately who understands and who doesn't.

Mike: I agree. That's why the staircase keeps happening, too. The greens keep getting one.

Anna: Hmmm…that's interesting, isn't it? So do you think we have all the ways on our staircase picture? Could there be any other ways? Talk to the person next to you about this.

Kimberly: There's no more ways…unless we make boxes that are all green or all red.

Anna: Who agrees with Kimberly? Thumbs up if you agree, thumbs down if you disagree. If you are not sure, wave your hand back and forth. *(Surveys the group.)* Seems like a few people aren't sure. Kimberly, can you convince them of your thinking? Let's put out some cubes. Here are 6 reds and 1 green. Show us how a red turns into a green each time. *(Kimberly demonstrates what she means, exchanging a red for a green each time.)* Peter and Jodi, did she convince you? *(They nod in agreement.)* So let's see then. We have 5 ways for the 6 box, 6 ways for the 7 box, 9 ways for the 10 box, and weren't there 4 ways for the 5 box? Seems as if there's a pattern here too! I wonder how many ways there are for a very big box, like a box of 20 apples? Or 30?

Asking for agreement or disagreement pushes everyone to commit, focus, and think.

Encouraging pattern recognition and then wondering "Will this happen again?" will promote inquiry, which is at the heart of what mathematicians do.

Reflections on the Day

Over the last several days, children have worked to examine the parts and wholes of numbers. What generalizations have they discussed?

It is helpful at this point to make a bulletin board and display the work. Children will enjoy revisiting and reminiscing about the ideas they constructed as they investigated, and they deserve to celebrate their many discoveries!

Part-Whole Bingo

Materials Needed

Number cubes (with dots, one through six)— two per pair of children

Part-Whole Bingo game boards (Appendix J)— one board per child

Connecting cubes— one small bin per pair of children

Student recording sheet for Part-Whole Bingo (Appendix K)—one per child

Now that the bunk bed and apple box investigations have come to a close, a new game, Part-Whole Bingo, is introduced to allow children to continue to explore arrangements and equivalence. This game promotes thinking about equivalence and the likelihood that combinations will appear. With the introduction of this game, children are being asked to consider pure number as a context and to use and extend the ideas they have been developing within the prior contexts of bunk beds and apple boxes.

Day Ten Outline

Developing the Context

☀ Model how to play Part-Whole Bingo.

☀ Note children's strategies as they play the game.

Developing the Context

Bring the children to a meeting area and have them sit in a circle. Play Part-Whole Bingo with another child in the center of the circle as a way to introduce the game to the class and model how the game is played.

☀ Model how to play Part-Whole Bingo.

☀ Note children's strategies as they play the game.

▣ Object of the Game

Part-Whole Bingo promotes the exploration of equivalence, and of decomposing and composing numbers by allowing children to cover equivalent arrangements, not just a match to the roll of the number cubes. What is covered must be justified as being equivalent to what was rolled. Because the objective is to cover the entire board, there is a built-in incentive to think about a variety of equivalent expressions.

▣ Directions for Playing

Have children play in pairs. Each player has a game board (Appendix J). Players take turns rolling the number cubes. The roll of the two number cubes combined determines the number of connecting cubes that each player can place on the board. For example, if one player rolls a 5 and a 2, each child takes seven connecting cubes and places them on his or her board.

Each player decides independently where to place the connecting cubes, and the two players' choices may be different. One child might cover all seven on the 7 track; the other child might cover the 5 and 2 tracks. It is also possible to cover tracks 2, 2, and 3, or tracks 6 and 1, instead. But each player per turn can place only seven connecting cubes in total, and no partial tracks may be used.

The objective is to eventually cover the entire game board. Play is cooperative rather than competitive; players are encouraged to help each other. The game ends when both boards are covered. Players can keep track of what they rolled and what they covered on the student recording sheet (Appendix K).

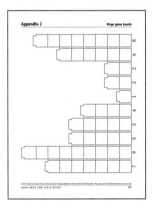

Reflections on the Unit

The mathematician Carl Friedrich Gauss (1808) wrote:

It is not knowledge but the act of learning, not possession but the act of getting there, which grants the greatest enjoyment. When I have clarified and exhausted a subject, then I turn away from it, in order to go into darkness again; the never satisfied man is so strange, if he has completed a structure, then it is not in order to dwell in it peacefully, but in order to begin another.

In this unit, your students have had many opportunities to explore the structure of number. They have composed and decomposed numbers, made equivalent arrangements, and developed strategies such as compensation. Initially they arranged children on bunk beds and explored the movement of children up and down the ladder while the total number of children stayed the same. Later they were challenged to exchange one apple for another and to analyze and reflect on whether they had found all possible arrangements. As a culmination, they were challenged to generalize about why the staircase representation occurred and to puzzle over why the total number of arrangements was always one less than the total number of apples in the box. Opportunities like these encourage them to develop ways to mathematize their lived worlds.

Sarah was excited. Saturday was finally here and tonight was her sleepover party! She had invited seven friends to spend the night and they were going to have fun playing on her new bunk beds. But the best part was that Aunt Kate was going to babysit! Aunt Kate was fun. She liked it when Sarah played tricks on her, and Sarah liked to play tricks!

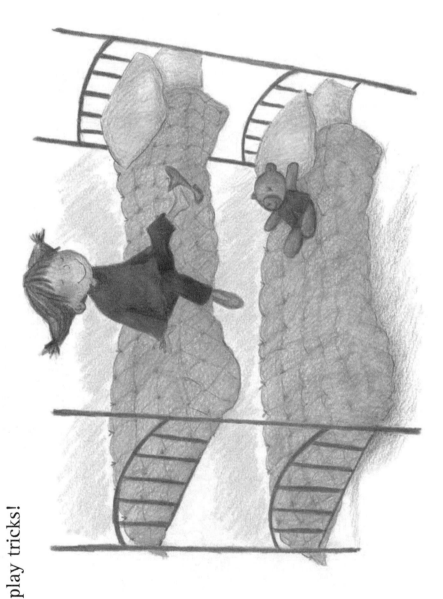

Bbrrring! Bbrrring! The doorbell rang! Sarah jumped down the stairs two at a time, yelling "Two, four, six, eight!" She ran to the door and opened it. Her friends all came tumbling in with sleeping bags and pillows, and backpacks filled with stuffed animals, pajamas and robes, slippers and toothbrushes.

"I brought some scary stories to read!" her best friend, Yolanda, exclaimed with a big smile as they ran to Sarah's room and jumped on the bunk bed. Four kids sat on the bottom bunk and two climbed up on the top bunk. Sarah and Yolanda climbed up on the top, too.

Aunt Kate smiled at the excited friends. "Would you like some popcorn?" she asked.

"Hmmm. Yum!" Sarah and her seven friends all yelled in unison.

"Yes, please! We want popcorn. We want popcorn. Four cups for the bottom bunk and four cups for the top bunk!"

"They will keep me busy tonight," Aunt Kate thought to herself and laughed as she went to the kitchen.

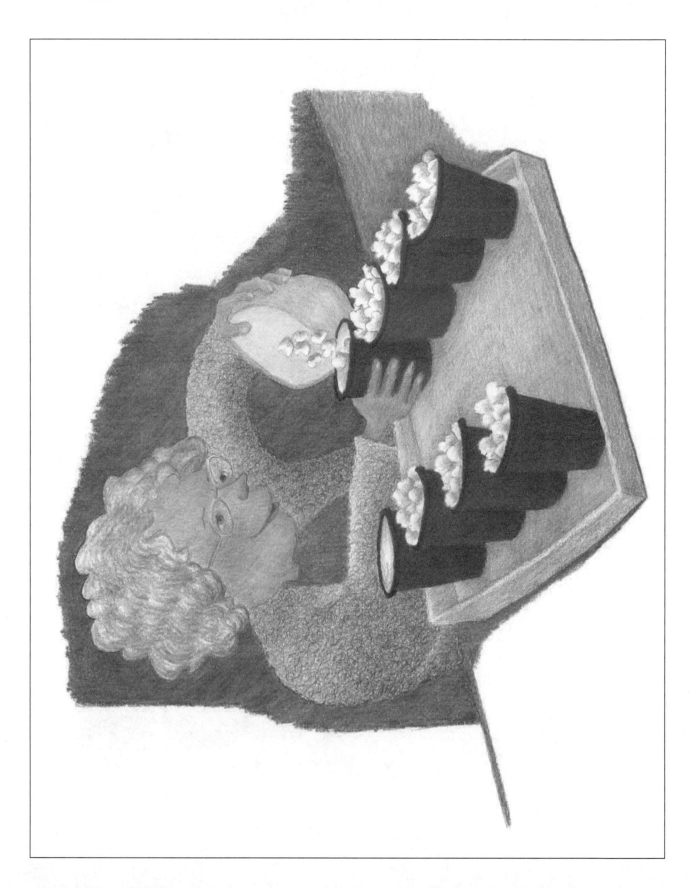

While the popcorn was popping, Aunt Kate laid out two rows of cups, four in each row, on a tray. "Four for the bottom bunk, four for the top bunk," she thought. When the popcorn finished popping, she filled the cups. Then up the steps she went.

"I hear her coming," Sarah exclaimed with a big smile and they all began to count. "One, two, three, four, five, six, seven, eight. Eight steps!" they yelled in unison. "The popcorn is coming!"

Aunt Kate chuckled as they counted each step, but when she got to the top she almost dropped the tray. This is what she saw.

"I've lost a kid!" Aunt Kate gasped in surprise.

The kids laughed and laughed. "No, we're all here. We just tricked you!"

"I'm down here now," Sarah said. She loved playing with Aunt Kate.

"Oh! Whew!" Aunt Kate said. "That's a relief!" And she passed out the big cups of popcorn. One, two, three, four, five, to the bottom, and then one, two, three, to the top. The kids all began to whisper and laugh about a new trick. "May we please have some juice?" they asked with glee.

Down the stairs Aunt Kate went. "One, two, three, four, five, six, seven, eight. Eight steps. Whew! I'm tired already," she thought with amusement. "Sarah does like to play tricks. She has me all confused! Now, how many cups of juice do I need? Let's see," she thought, "there were five kids on the bottom and three kids on the top. How many is that?" She laid out the cups, five and three, on a tray. She poured the juice into the cups, and back up the steps she went.

"Here she comes," Sarah reported.

"One, two, three, four, five, six, seven, eight. Eight steps!" all the kids yelled. "The juice is coming!"

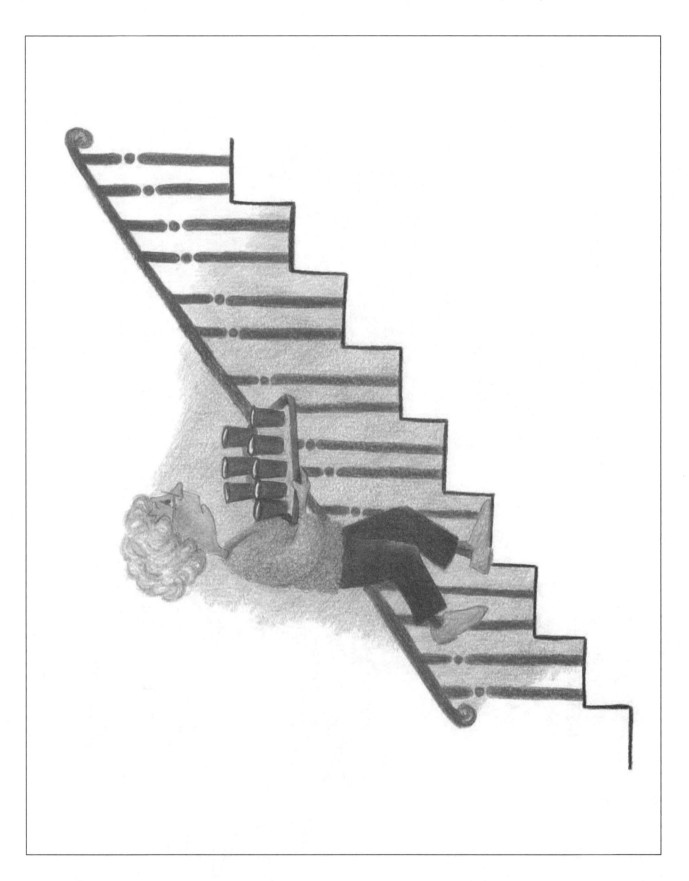

When she got to Sarah's room, Aunt Kate almost dropped the tray.
This is what she saw.

"I've gained a kid!" Aunt Kate exclaimed in disbelief.
"We tricked you, we tricked you!" the kids howled in laughter, very pleased with themselves.

"How could that be?" Aunt Kate thought and thought. "What were they doing?" She passed out the juice to the kids on the bottom, counting ever so carefully, "One, two, three, four, five, six." Next she did the top, "One, two." It was just enough! Five and three was just the right amount for six kids on the bottom and two kids on the top! Aunt Kate was puzzled. How is this happening? Shaking her head, she muttered, "I'll go get some napkins."

Down the stairs Aunt Kate went again. "One, two, three, four, five, six, seven, eight. Eight steps!" How many napkins did she need? What would help her remember how many kids there were? "Let's see," she thought, "there were six kids on the bottom and two kids on the top. Before that it was five on the bottom and three on the top, and before that it was four on the bottom and four on the top. But I don't think there are any other ways they can trick me, so this time I'll bring up six napkins for the kids on the bottom and two napkins for the kids on the top and then I can rest!"

Is Aunt Kate right? Does she have the right number of napkins? How many ways can the kids trick her?

To make a class-size arithmetic rack, find a large piece of cardboard, about three feet by one and a half feet. Punch four holes, two on each side, through the cardboard, approximately six inches apart top to bottom, but two feet across. Using wire or thin rope (such as clothesline), string twenty beads in two rows of ten each (five of each color) as in the illustration below. Thread the wire or rope through the holes and twist or tie in the back. [**Note:** If you use wire, it is possible to use connecting cubes in place of beads]

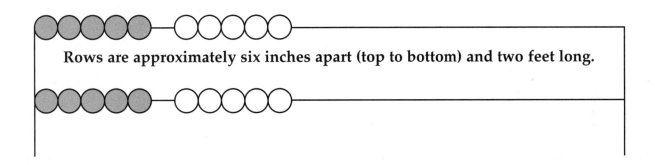

Rows are approximately six inches apart (top to bottom) and two feet long.

Individual arithmetic racks can be made in a similar fashion to the class-size arithmetic rack. Just use a smaller piece of cardboard, about four inches by twelve inches. Use shoelaces in place of wire and make sure that the beads you use are small enough to move easily along the shoelaces.

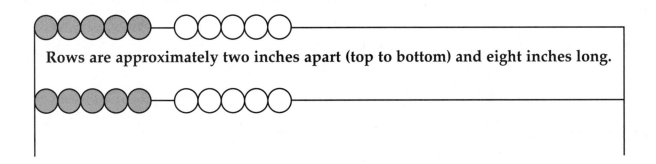

Rows are approximately two inches apart (top to bottom) and eight inches long.

Visit www.contextsforlearning.com for information on where to purchase arithmetic racks.

Name _____ Date _____

Directions: Cut the strips out of red and white oaktag, making enough strips to include sufficient velcro places for the number of children in your class. Align in *complete* rows of ten: 5 red and white in each row.

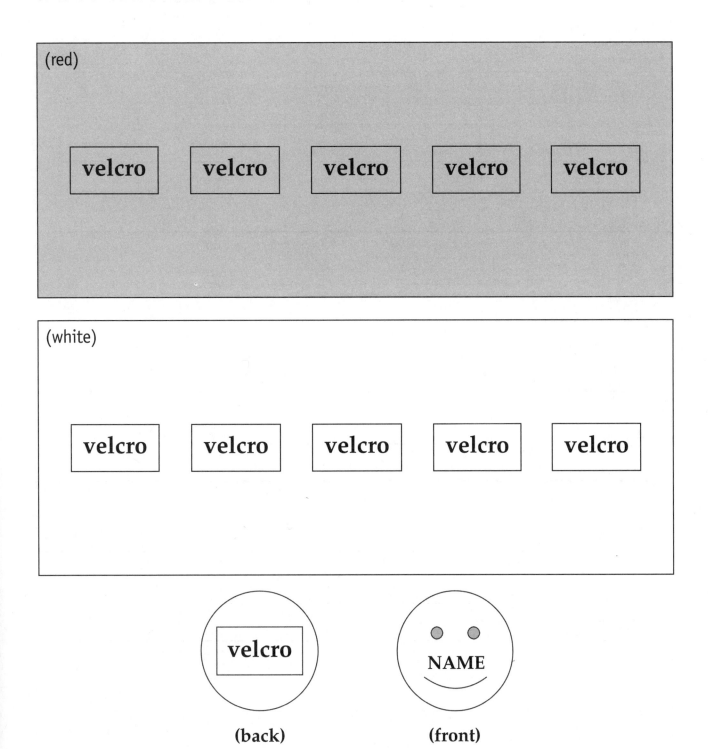

(red)

velcro   velcro   velcro   velcro   velcro

(white)

velcro   velcro   velcro   velcro   velcro

velcro

NAME

(back)   **(front)**

Use popsicle sticks for bodies if you wish.

Student recording sheet for Up and Down the Ladder

Player One   Player Two   Name _____

BUNK BEDS AND APPLE BOXES

■ These cards can be made more durable by pasting them on oaktag and laminating them.

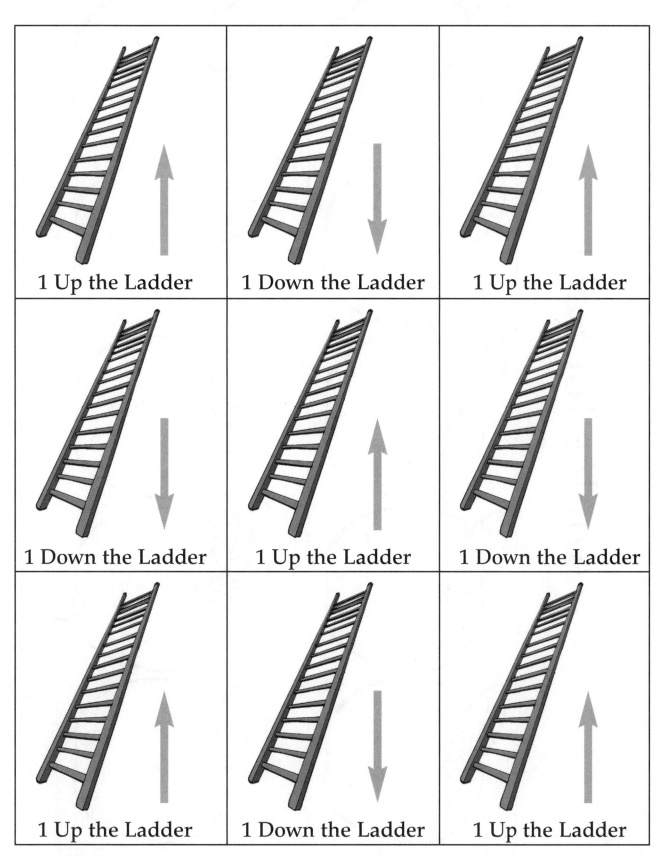

1 Up the Ladder	1 Down the Ladder	1 Up the Ladder
1 Down the Ladder	1 Up the Ladder	1 Down the Ladder
1 Up the Ladder	1 Down the Ladder	1 Up the Ladder

Apples for Sale

Student recording sheet for the apple boxes investigation

Names _____ Date _____

Names _____ Date _____

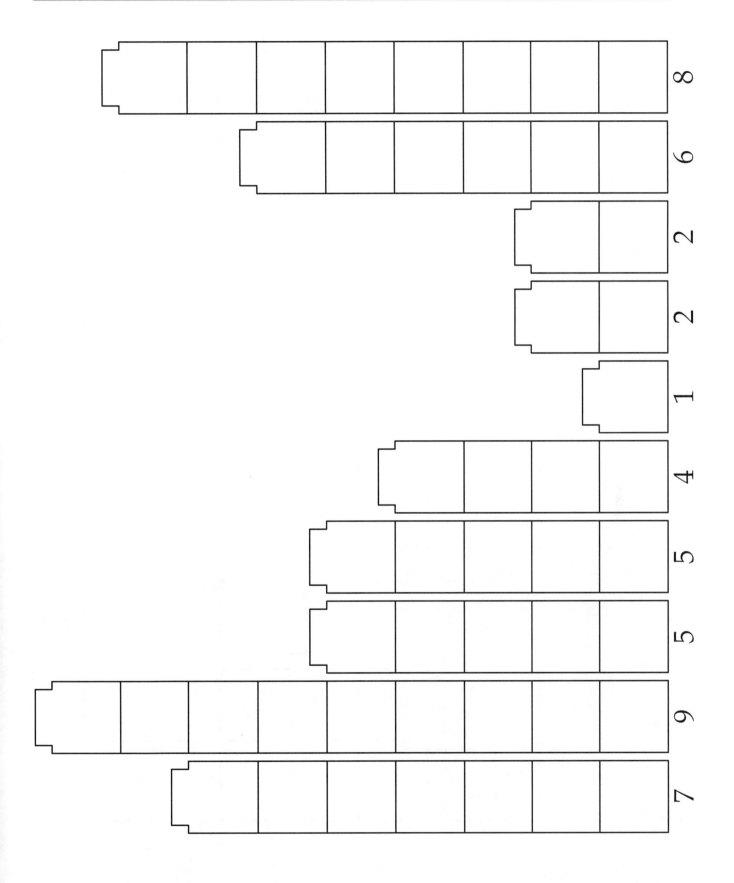

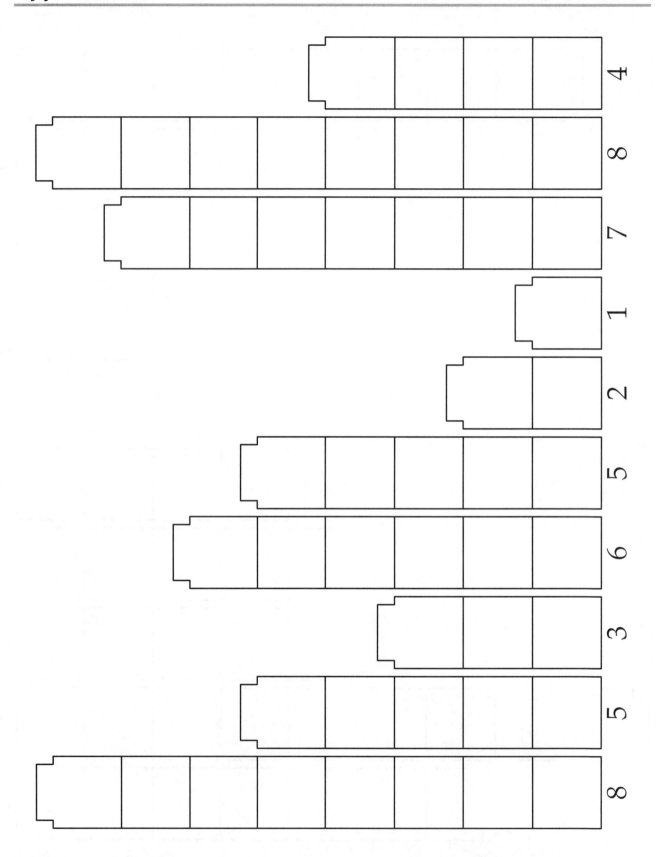

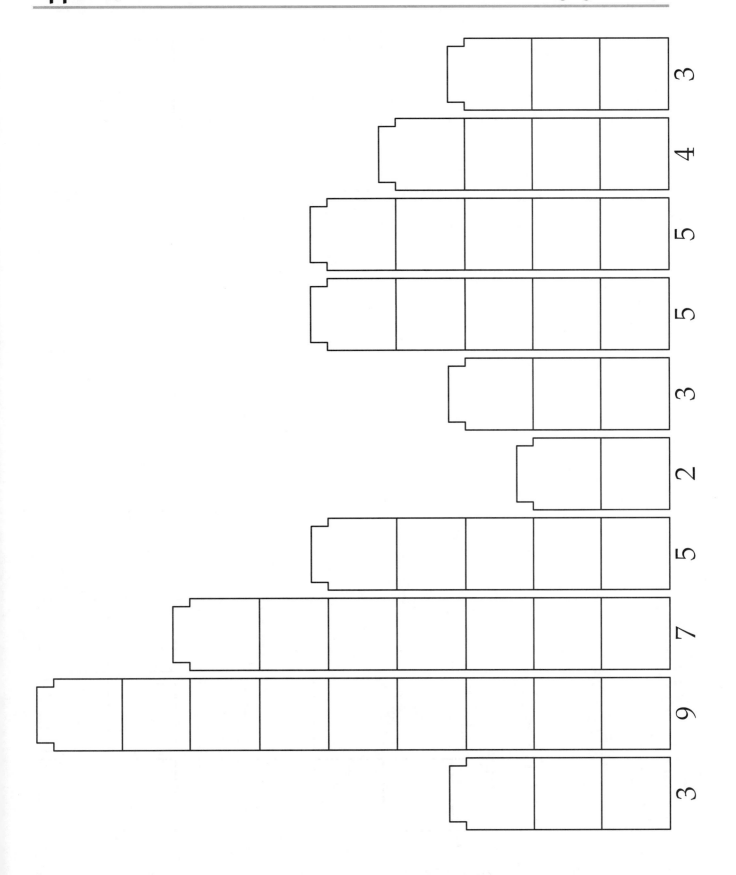

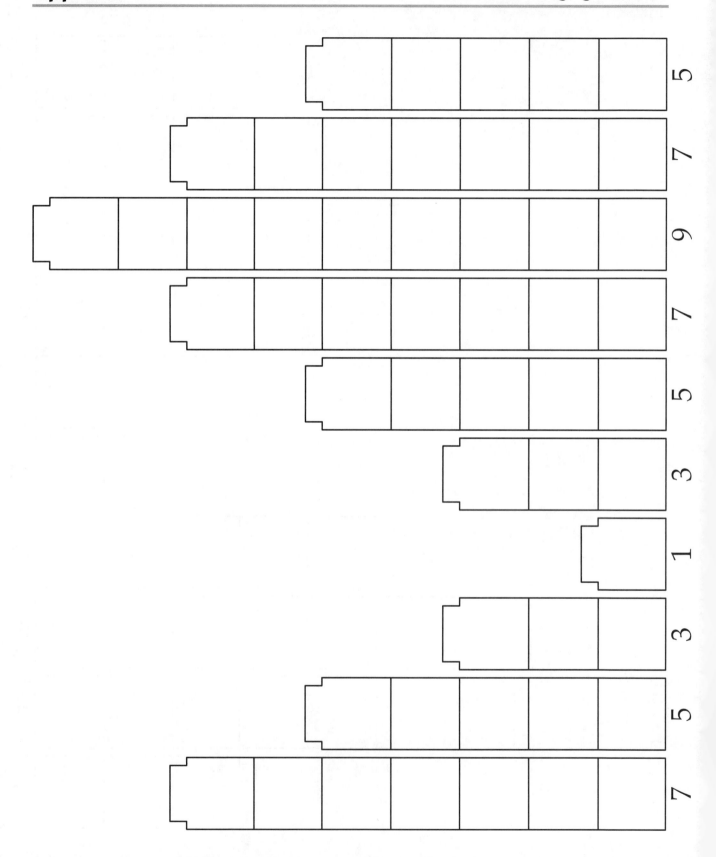

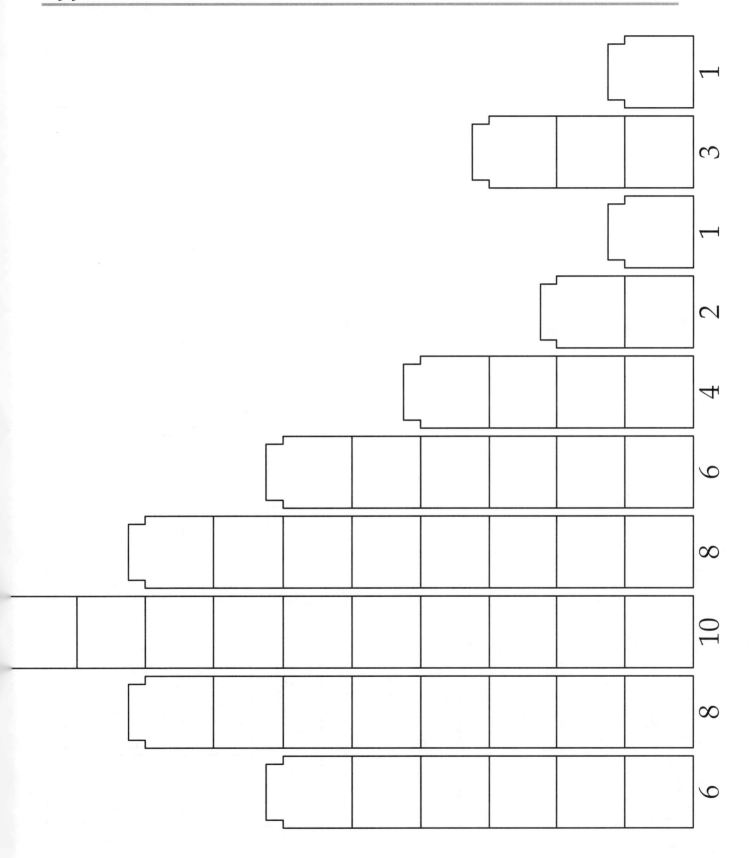

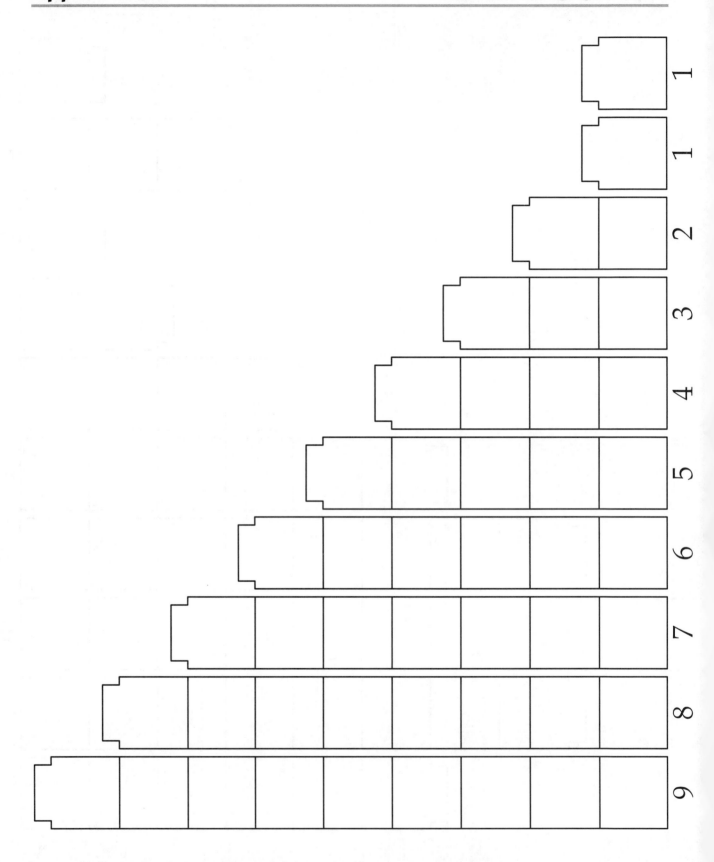

1
1
2
3
4
5
6
7
8
9

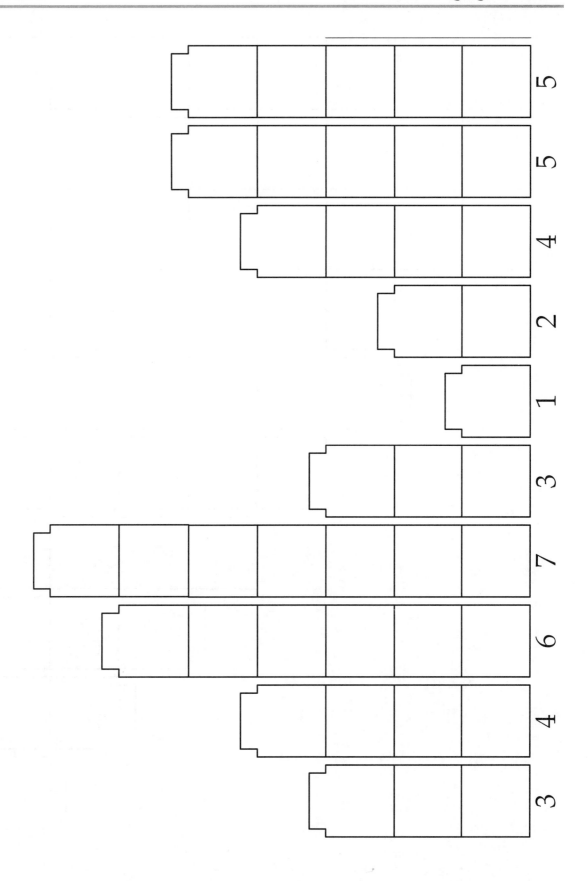

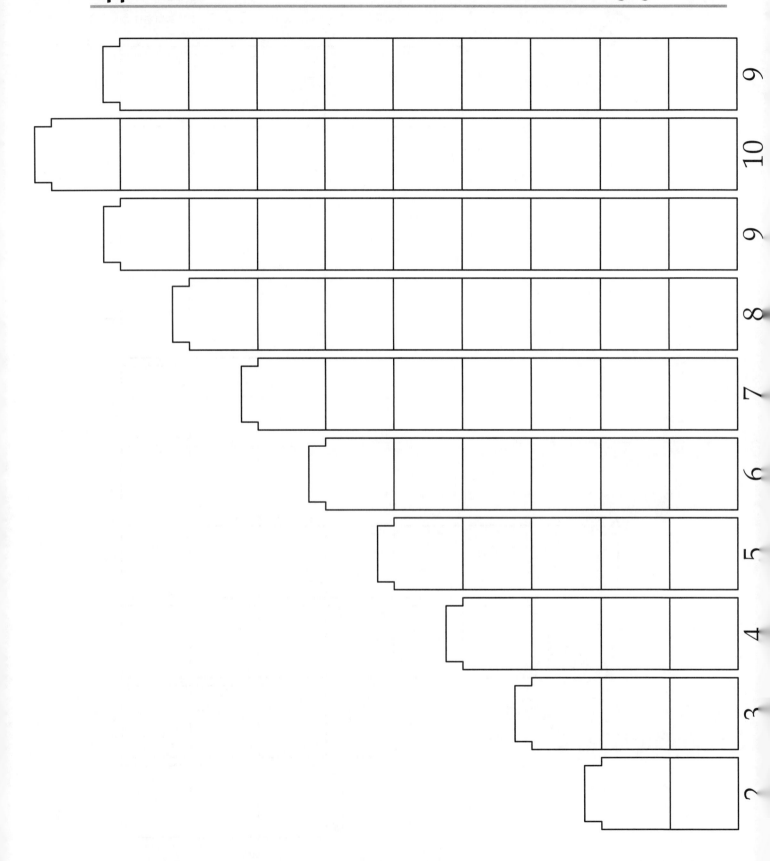

	Numbers rolled	Tracks I covered
1.		
2.		
3.		
4.		
5.		
6.		
7.		
8.		
9.		
10.		
11.		
12.		
13.		
14.		
15.		